S0-AGL-143

DISCARD

The new Solar System

Uranus

Robin Birch

CHELSEA CLUBHOUSE

An Imprint of Chelsea House Publishers

This edition published in 2008 in the United States of America by Chelsea Clubhouse, a division of
Chelsea House Publishers.

Chelsea Clubhouse
An imprint of Chelsea House Publishers
132 West 31st Street
New York, NY 10001

Chelsea Clubhouse books are available at special discounts when purchased in bulk quantities for
businesses, associations, institutions, or sales promotions. Please call our Special Sales Department in
New York at (212) 967-8800 or (800) 322-8755.

You can find Chelsea Clubhouse on the World Wide Web at: http://www.chelseahouse.com

First published in 2004 by
MACMILLAN EDUCATION AUSTRALIA PTY LTD
15–19 Claremont Street, South Yarra, 3141

Visit our Web site at www.macmillan.com.au or go directly to www.macmillanlibrary.com.au

Associated companies and representatives throughout the world.

Library of Congress Cataloging-in-Publication Data

Birch, Robin.
  Uranus / Robin Birch. — 2nd ed.
  p. cm. — (The new solar system)
  Includes index.
  ISBN 978-1-60413-214-4
  1. Uranus (Planet) —Juvenile literature. I. Title.
  QB681.B57 2008
  523.47—dc22

                                                2007051543

Edited by Anna Fern
Text and cover design by Cristina Neri, Canary Graphic Design
Photo research by Legend Images
Illustrations by Melissa Webb, Noisypics

Printed in the United States of America

Acknowledgements
The author and publisher are grateful to the following for permission to reproduce copyright material:

Cover photograph of Uranus courtesy of NASA/JPL.

Australian Picture Library/Corbis, pp. 5 (both), 12, 23, 25; Calvin J. Hamilton, pp. 4 (left), 7, 11, 21, 22;
Walter Myers/www.arcadiastreet.com, p. 10; NASA/JPL, pp. 16 (left), 24; Photodisc, p. 28;
Photolibrary.com/SPL, pp. 6, 13, 14, 15, 16 (right), 17, 18, 19, 20, 26, 27, 29.

Background and border images courtesy of Photodisc, and view of Uranus courtesy of NASA/JPL.

While every care has been taken to trace and acknowledge copyright, the publisher offers their apologies
for any accidental infringement where copyright has proved untraceable. Where the attempt has been
unsuccessful, the publisher welcomes information that would redress the situation.

Please note
At the time of printing, the Internet addresses appearing in this book were correct. Owing to the dynamic
nature of the Internet, however, we cannot guarantee that all these addresses will remain correct.

Contents

Glossary words

When you see a word printed in bold, **like this**, you can look up its meaning in the glossary on page 31.

Discovering Uranus

The **planet** Uranus is just visible to our eyes at certain times, if we know exactly where to look. Usually, a **telescope** is needed to see Uranus.

Uranus was discovered by William Herschel, in 1781. Herschel was scanning the sky with his telescope, looking for faraway objects. He found a small dot which was not a **comet**, and which was not listed as a **star**. This meant the dot would probably be an unknown planet. Uranus was the first planet to be discovered with a telescope.

▼ The planet Uranus

William Herschel was born in Germany, in 1738. He became a musician and moved to England, where he taught music and studied mathematics. Then he started building telescopes and became more and more interested in **astronomy**.

▲ This is the symbol for Uranus.

▲ The god Uranus

The word "planet" means "wanderer." Stars always make the same pattern in the sky. Planets slowly change their location in the sky, compared to the stars around them. This is why planets were called "wanderers."

▶ *Voyager 2*

Uranus has five large **moons** and many small ones. The first two moons to be discovered were found by Herschel in 1787. They are the largest two moons, Titania and Oberon.

The only **space probe** to visit Uranus was *Voyager 2*, in 1986. It took close-up photographs of Uranus.

Uranus was named after the Greek god of the sky. The god Uranus was the father of the god Cronos (another name for Saturn).

The Seventh Planet

The planet Uranus **revolves** around the Sun, along with seven other planets and many other bodies. The Sun, planets, and other bodies together are called the solar system. Uranus is the seventh planet from the Sun.

There are eight planets in the solar system. Mercury, Venus, Earth, and Mars are made of rock. They are the smallest planets, and are closest to the Sun. Jupiter, Saturn, Uranus, and Neptune are made mainly of **gas** and liquid. They are the largest planets, and are farthest from the Sun.

The solar system also has dwarf planets. The first three bodies to be called dwarf planets were Ceres, Pluto, and Eris. Ceres is an asteroid. Pluto and Eris are known as **trans-Neptunian objects**.

A planet is a body that:

- orbits the Sun
- is nearly round in shape
- has cleared the area around its orbit (its **gravity** is strong enough)

A dwarf planet is a body that:

- orbits the Sun
- is nearly round in shape
- has not cleared the area around its orbit
- is not a **moon**

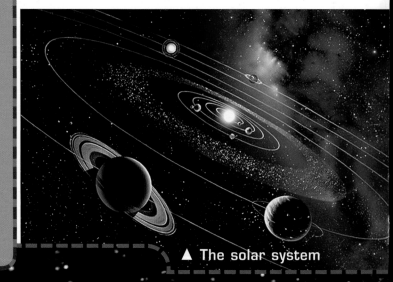

▲ The solar system

There are also many small solar system bodies in the solar system. These include asteroids, comets, trans-Neptunian objects, and other small bodies which have not been called dwarf planets.

Asteroids are made of rock. Most of them, including dwarf planet Ceres, orbit the Sun in a path called the asteroid belt. The asteroid belt lies between the orbits of Mars and Jupiter. Comets are made mainly of ice and rock. When their orbits bring them close to the Sun, comets grow a tail. Trans-Neptunian objects are icy, and orbit the Sun farther out on average than Neptune.

▶ The eight planets are Mercury, Venus, Earth, Mars, Jupiter, Saturn, Uranus, and Neptune.

The solar system is about 4,600 million years old.

Planet	Average distance from Sun	
Mercury	35,960,000 miles	(57,910,000 kilometers)
Venus	67,190,000 miles	(108,200,000 kilometers)
Earth	92,900,000 miles	(149,600,000 kilometers)
Mars	141,550,000 miles	(227,940,000 kilometers)
Jupiter	483,340,000 miles	(778,330,000 kilometers)
Saturn	887,660,000 miles	(1,429,400,000 kilometers)
Uranus	1,782,880,000 miles	(2,870,990,000 kilometers)
Neptune	2,796,000,000 miles	(4,504,000,000 kilometers)

The name "solar system" comes from the word "Sol," the Latin name for the Sun.

On Uranus

As it travels around the Sun, the gas-giant planet Uranus spins on its **axis**.

Rotation and Revolution

Uranus **rotates** on its axis once every 17.24 Earth hours. Compared to other planets, Uranus is lying on its side, with its axis tilted over by 97.9 degrees. It is possible that Uranus spins on its side because it was hit by something very big when it was young.

Uranus takes 84 Earth years to orbit the Sun once, which is the length of one year on Uranus. The orbit of Uranus is almost a perfect circle. The Sun's gravity keeps Uranus revolving around it.

Uranus has very unusual seasons because it is lying right over on its side. When one **pole** has summer, it is one long day. The opposite pole has one long night.

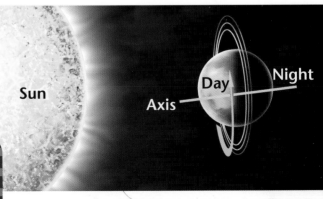

▲ Uranus rotates as it revolves around the Sun.

Astronomers disagree on which part of Uranus is the north pole and which is the south pole, because Uranus is lying on its side.

Southern Winter

Northern Summer

Sun

Southern Summer

Northern Winter

▲ The seasons on Uranus

It took astronomers a long time to figure out if Uranus changes with the seasons. This is because the seasons last for 21 years each.

Seasons

Each of the four seasons on Uranus lasts for about 21 years. In the northern summer on Uranus, the Sun shines almost directly on the north pole for about 21 years. Then the Sun shines on the **equator** for about 21 years. In the southern summer, the Sun shines directly on the south pole for about 21 years. Then the Sun shines on the equator again for 21 years.

The unusual seasons on Uranus should make the summer area hot and the winter area cold. However, the seasons make very little difference to the temperature. The temperature at the top of the clouds is usually about –350 degrees Fahrenheit (–214 degrees Celsius).

Size and Structure

Uranus is 31,744 miles (51,118 kilometers) in **diameter** at the equator. It is the third largest planet in the solar system and is about four times wider than Earth. Uranus is the fourth heaviest planet. (Neptune is heavier, even though Neptune is a little smaller in size than Uranus.)

Uranus is made mainly of rock and icy substances. It is about 15 percent hydrogen and has a little helium. Uranus is called a gas giant because it has no solid ground to land on. The planets Jupiter, Saturn, and Neptune are also gas giants.

▼ Compare the size of Uranus and Earth.

Uranus is slightly flattened at the poles. This is probably because it spins very fast, and the substances inside it can move around easily.

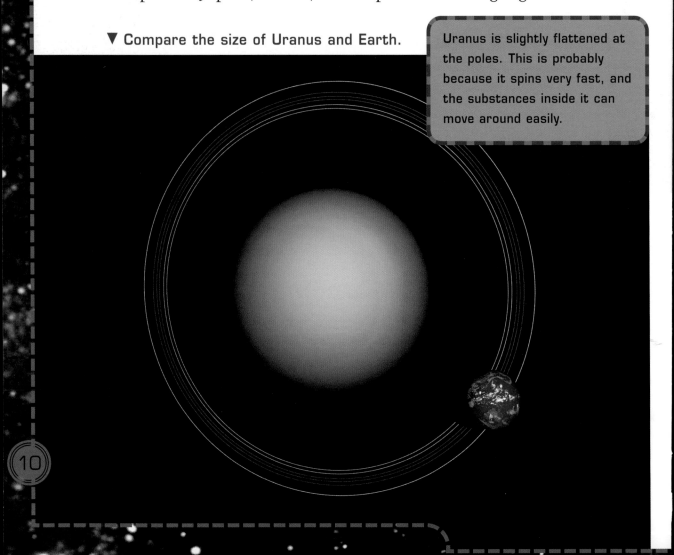

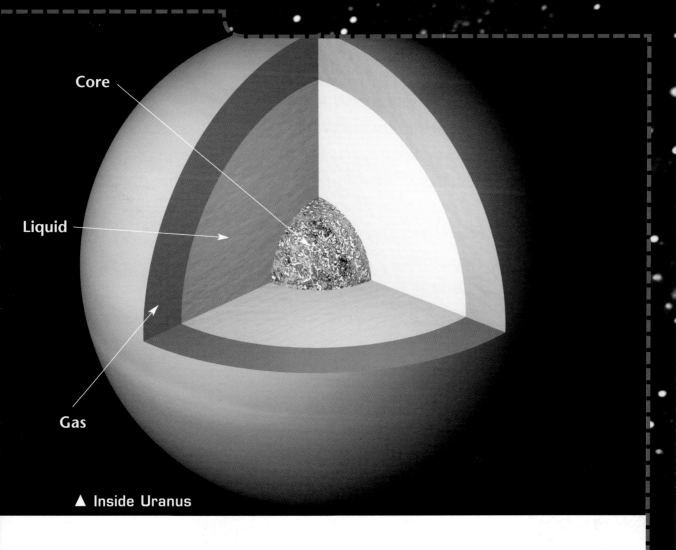

Core

Liquid

Gas

▲ Inside Uranus

Uranus has an **atmosphere** of gases around it. The atmosphere is made up of 83 percent hydrogen, 15 percent helium and 2 percent methane. The methane gives Uranus its green-blue color.

Below the atmosphere, Uranus has a wide layer of gases which are so tightly squeezed together that they act like icy liquid. This layer contains mainly the substances water, methane, and ammonia. There are probably hard, rocky, and icy substances at the center of Uranus, making a **core**. It is possible that these hard substances are spread around inside Uranus, instead of being in a definite core.

Clouds

The first close-up pictures of Uranus did not show obvious clouds. Uranus looked the same greenish-blue color all over. Now we know that Uranus has bands of clouds which blow quickly around the planet. It is possible that the upper atmosphere covers clouds below it, so they are hard to see.

Winds blow around the equator of Uranus at up to 225 miles (360 kilometers) per hour. Winds blow in the opposite direction on either side of the equator. These winds blow at 95 to 360 miles (150 to 580 kilometers) per hour.

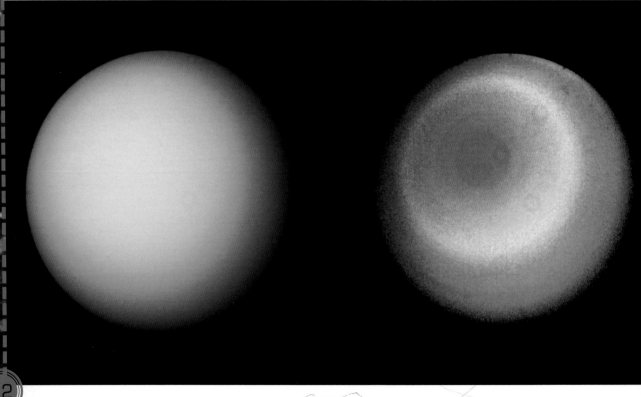

▲ Two views of Uranus. The one on the right shows bands of cloud at one of the poles in false color.

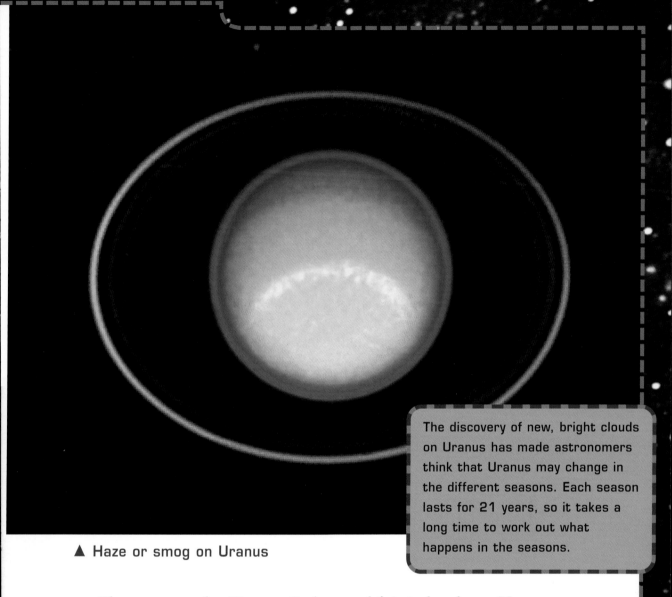

▲ Haze or smog on Uranus

The discovery of new, bright clouds on Uranus has made astronomers think that Uranus may change in the different seasons. Each season lasts for 21 years, so it takes a long time to work out what happens in the seasons.

The space probe *Voyager 2* observed faint clouds on Uranus in 1986. They were being blown by fast winds in the southern **hemisphere**. *Voyager 2* also found a layer of haze or smog high up in the atmosphere, at the pole that was lit by the Sun.

The *Hubble Space Telescope* photographed about 20 bright clouds on Uranus in 1998. These clouds were probably made of crystals of the substance methane. They may have formed from methane gas which had bubbled up from deep in the atmosphere.

Giving Off Light

Jupiter, Saturn, and Neptune all give off more heat than they receive from the Sun. Uranus does not produce heat like these other gas-giant planets do. Uranus only reflects the heat it has received from the Sun.

Uranus gives off large amounts of **ultraviolet light** from the part lit up by the Sun. This was discovered by the space probe *Voyager 2*. The astronomers operating *Voyager 2* called the light given off "day-glow."

▼ These pictures of Uranus have been colored to show differences between parts of the atmosphere.

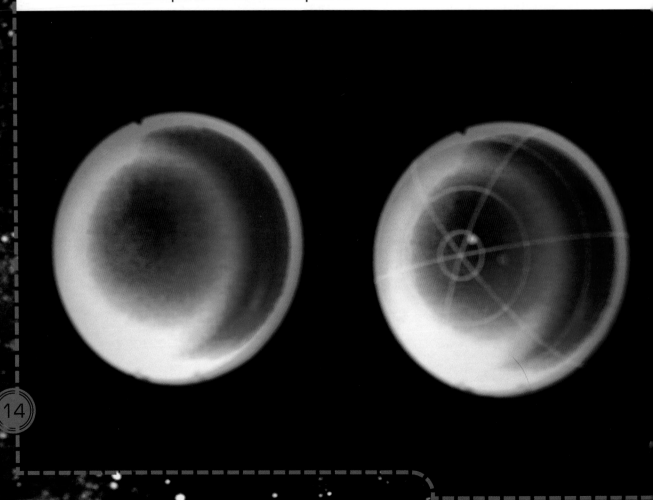

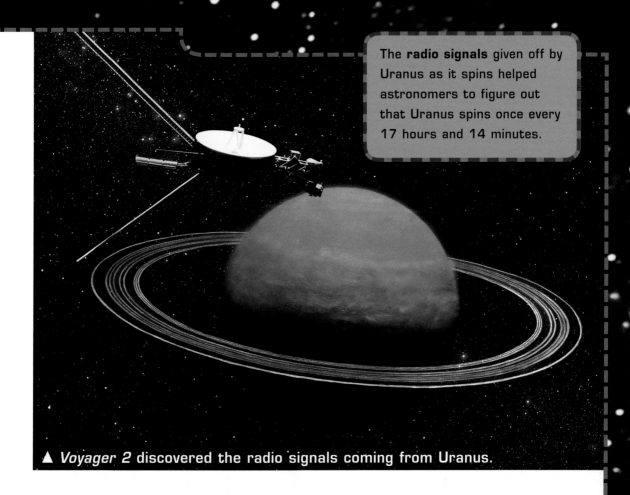

▲ *Voyager 2* discovered the radio signals coming from Uranus.

Magnetic Field

Uranus gives off radio signals. They were discovered by *Voyager 2* as it got near Uranus. The radio signals show that Uranus has a **magnetic field** in parts of space around it. The magnetic field traps **charged** particles floating in space. When Uranus spins, the magnetic field containing the charged particles also spins, making the radio signals.

The charged particles trapped in Uranus's magnetic field form **radiation belts.** These are very strong and would damage electronic equipment that came near. The radiation belts possibly made the rings and inner moons of Uranus dark in color.

Rings and Moons

Uranus has 27 moons circling around it, as well as 13 rings of dust and rock.

Rings

Uranus has dark rings around it which do not show up in ordinary photographs. Most were discovered in 1977 and were the first rings to be found on a planet besides Saturn. This discovery was very important at the time, because it showed that other planets besides Saturn could have rings. We now know that all the gas-giant planets have rings.

▼ Uranus with its closer rings and some of its moons

The rings of Uranus are upright compared to the rings of other planets. This is because Uranus lies on its side and the rings rotate around the planet's equator.

► A closer look at the rings around Uranus

▲ The inner rings
of Uranus

Astronomers have discovered that
Uranus's rings wobble like an unbalanced
wheel. The wobble is possibly caused by
the gravity of Uranus's moons, which
may pull on the rings.

Uranus has 13 rings. There is an inner group of 11 rings
and two more rings twice as far away from Uranus.

The rings are made of dust, pebbles, and larger lumps. Some
lumps are up to 33 feet (10 meters) in diameter. The inside ring
is wide and cloudy, and all the other rings are dark and narrow.
The brightest ring is the Epsilon ring, which is the eleventh
ring from Uranus.

Moons

Uranus has at least 27 moons.

- There are 13 very small, dark moons fairly close to the planet, between 31,000 and 60,000 miles (50,000 and 98,000 kilometers) away.
- Farther out, there are five large moons, between 81,000 and 362,000 miles (130,000 and 583,000 kilometers) away.
- Even farther out are nine more small moons, between 2,657,000 and 12,987,000 miles (4,276,000 and 20,901,000 kilometers) away.

Most of the moons orbit around Uranus in an almost perfect circle. The outside nine moons have oval orbits. Like the rings around Uranus, the orbits of the moons are upright because Uranus is lying on its side.

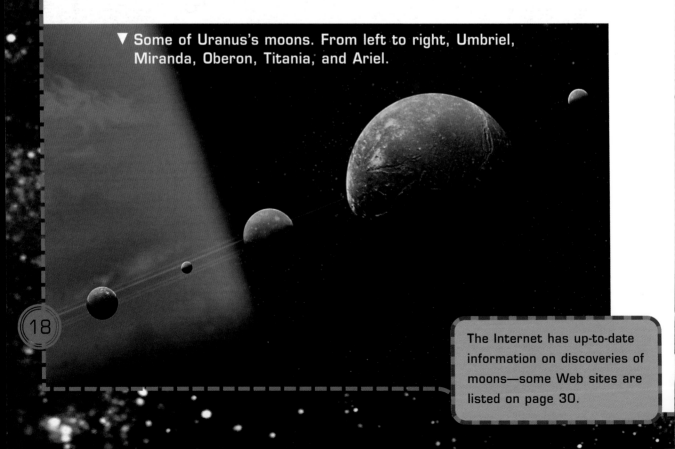

▼ Some of Uranus's moons. From left to right, Umbriel, Miranda, Oberon, Titania, and Ariel.

The Internet has up-to-date information on discoveries of moons—some Web sites are listed on page 30.

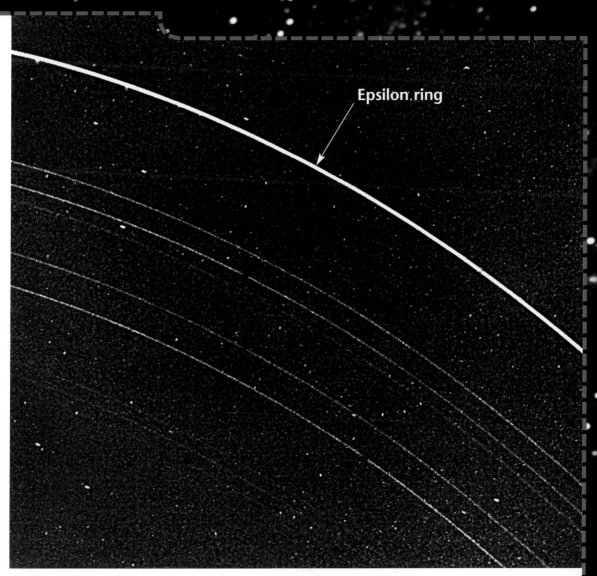

Epsilon ring

▲ The bright Epsilon ring, which has two shepherd moons

Shepherd Moons

Two of the small inner moons of Uranus are shepherd moons. Shepherd moons orbit near a ring and help to keep the particles in the ring in place. They stop particles from falling towards the planet, or from flying away from the planet.

The moons Cordelia and Ophelia are shepherd moons for the outside ring, the Epsilon ring. Cordelia orbits just inside the Epsilon ring. Ophelia orbits just outside the Epsilon ring.

Miranda

Miranda is the closest large moon to Uranus, about 80,000 miles (130,000 kilometers) away. It is also the smallest of the large moons, with a diameter of 293 miles (472 kilometers). Miranda is made up of about 50 percent frozen water and 50 percent rocky substances. It takes Miranda 1.4 Earth days to orbit Uranus once.

Miranda was discovered in 1948. In 1986, the space probe *Voyager 2* flew close to Miranda on its way to Neptune. Astronomers were very surprised by the pictures of Miranda sent back by *Voyager 2*. Miranda turned out to be the most interesting of all Uranus's large moons.

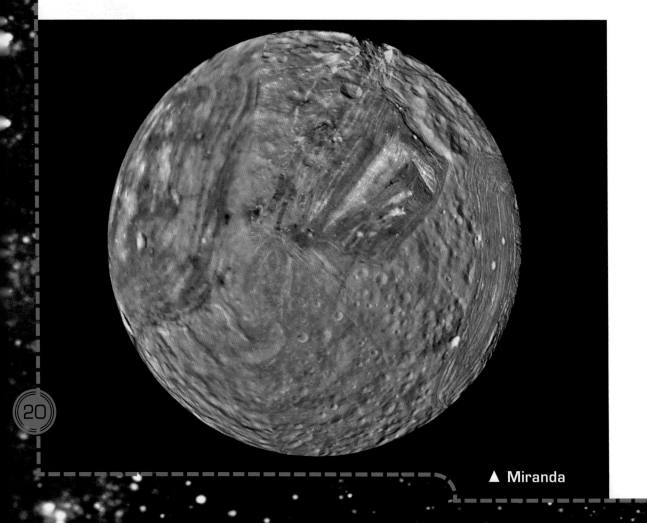

▲ Miranda

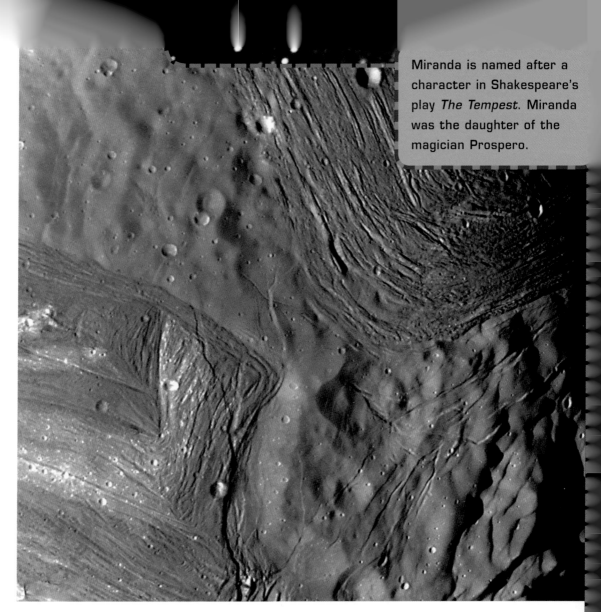

▲ Markings on Miranda

Miranda has a surface that is all mixed up. Miranda is thickly covered with **craters**, where asteroids have hit it. It has enormous canyons up to 12 miles (20 kilometers) deep, as well as other grooves and valleys. Miranda has soaring cliffs—one cliff is more than 3 miles (5 kilometers) high.

Miranda has a mixture of old and young surfaces. The features may have been caused by partly melted ice coming up to the surface from below, and freezing solid.

Ariel

Ariel is the second large moon from Uranus. It is 119,000 miles (191,000 kilometers) away from Uranus. Ariel is 719 miles (1,158 kilometers) in diameter. It is Uranus's brightest moon. It was discovered in 1851. It takes Ariel 2.5 Earth days to orbit Uranus once.

Ariel is made up of about 50 percent frozen water and 50 percent rock. The surface has long valleys and canyons which criss-cross it. Some older parts of Ariel have craters, where asteroids have hit it. The craters are 3 to 6 miles (5 to 10 kilometers) in diameter. Other parts are younger. Liquids have come to the surface and frozen solid, making a smooth surface. Some of the valleys have floors smoothed over in this way.

◀ Ariel

The valleys on Ariel can be hundreds of miles long and more than 6 miles (10 kilometers) deep. The valleys could be cracks formed when Ariel cooled down and froze, when it was young.

▲ Umbriel

Ariel is named after a naughty spirit in Shakespeare's play *The Tempest.* Umbriel is the name of a character in a poem by Alexander Pope.

Umbriel

Umbriel is the third large moon from Uranus. It was discovered in 1851. Umbriel is 730 miles (1,170 kilometers) in diameter and takes 4.1 Earth days to travel around Uranus. Umbriel is 165,000 miles (266,000 kilometers) away from Uranus.

Umbriel is made of about 50 percent rock and 50 percent frozen water. It is covered with craters, many of them large. Umbriel is much the same all over. It is a rather dark moon and only reflects about half as much sunlight as Ariel. There is a bright ring at the top of Umbriel nicknamed the "fluorescent cheerio." It is probably the floor of a crater.

Titania

Titania is the fourth large moon from Uranus. It was discovered in 1787. Titania is Uranus's largest moon, with a diameter of 980 miles (1,578 kilometers). It is 271,000 miles (436,000 kilometers) away from Uranus and orbits Uranus in 8.7 Earth days.

Titania is made of about 50 percent frozen water and 50 percent rock. The surface has some large craters and many small craters, made when asteroids hit Titania. Very long valleys criss-cross the surface. The valleys are probably cracks that formed when Titania was cooling down, when it was young. The outside would have cooled down, hardened and shrunk before the inside did, making cracks in the surface.

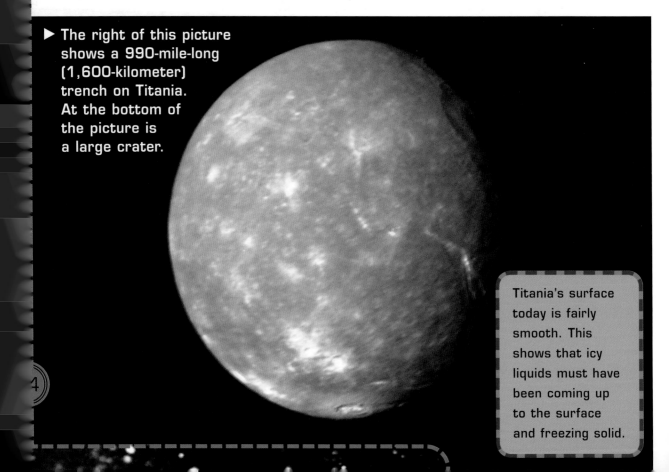

▶ The right of this picture shows a 990-mile-long (1,600-kilometer) trench on Titania. At the bottom of the picture is a large crater.

Titania's surface today is fairly smooth. This shows that icy liquids must have been coming up to the surface and freezing solid.

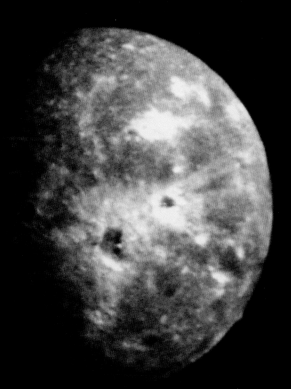

▲ This picture of Oberon shows large craters at the center, with some rays. On the lower right edge is a 4-mile-high (6-kilometer) mountain.

Oberon

Oberon is the farthest large moon from Uranus, about 362,000 miles (583,000 kilometers) away. Its diameter is 946 miles (1,523 kilometers). Oberon orbits Uranus in 13.5 Earth days. It was discovered in 1787.

Oberon is made of about 50 percent rock and 50 percent frozen water. It has probably stayed much the same since it formed. Oberon is covered with craters where asteroids have hit. Some craters have pale rays coming from them. These are streaks of dust thrown up when asteroids hit Oberon, making the craters. Some crater floors are dark, possibly from dirty water welling up from below.

Exploring Uranus

Uranus has been visited by one spacecraft, *Voyager 2*. The spacecraft had no people on board, but was operated by astronomers on Earth by sending and receiving radio signals. This type of spacecraft is called a space probe.

Voyager 2 was launched in 1977. It visited Jupiter in 1979, Saturn in 1981, Uranus in 1986 and Neptune in 1989. *Voyager 2* is on its way out of the solar system. Astronomers will keep getting information from it until about 2030.

◀ *Voyager 2*

Voyager 2 uses its dish-shaped antennas to send radio signals back to Earth.

▶ This photo of Uranus was taken by *Voyager 2.*

Voyager 2 Discoveries

In 1986, *Voyager 2* took the first close-up pictures of Uranus. They showed a planet which was mainly the same color all over, with some faint clouds in the southern hemisphere. *Voyager 2* discovered that Uranus's equator is about the same temperature as its poles.

    Voyager 2 discovered 10 of Uranus's small moons. It also took pictures of Uranus's five large moons, which showed the surfaces for the first time and revealed how the moons are different from each other. *Voyager 2* discovered details in Uranus's known rings and also discovered two new rings. *Voyager 2* confirmed that Uranus had a magnetic field which was large and unusual.

Hubble Space Telescope

The *Hubble Space Telescope (HST)* is a telescope which orbits Earth. The *HST* gets a clearer view of stars and planets than telescopes on Earth because it is above Earth's atmosphere. The *HST* carries cameras, and instruments for detecting heat and studying light. The telescope was sent into space on board the space shuttle *Discovery* in 1990. When *Discovery* reached space, the *HST* was released to orbit Earth on its own.

The *HST* has found new bright clouds speeding around Uranus. This shows that the weather on Uranus is more interesting than was once thought.

▼ The *Hubble Space Telescope* above Earth

▲ An artist's impression of explorers on Miranda

Questions about Uranus

There is still a lot to learn about Uranus. One day, astronomers hope to find out the answers to questions such as these:

🐜 Why is Uranus tilted on its side? Is it because it collided with something big?

🐜 Why does Uranus not give off more heat than it receives from the Sun, like the other gas-giant planets?

🐜 Why does Uranus contain a lot less hydrogen and helium than Jupiter and Saturn?

🐜 Will Uranus have different weather as it goes through its different seasons? The *HST* will be used to see if the weather changes.

Uranus Fact Summary

Distance from Sun (average)	1,782,880,000 miles (2,870,990,000 kilometers)
Diameter (at equator)	31,744 miles (51,118 kilometers)
Mass	14.54 times Earth's mass
Density	1.3 times the density of water
Gravity	.89 times Earth's gravity
Temperature (top of clouds)	– 350 degrees Fahrenheit (–214 degrees Celsius)
Rotation on axis	17.24 Earth hours
Revolution	84 Earth years
Number of moons	21 plus

Web Sites

www.solarviews.com/eng/uranus.htm
Uranus

www.nineplanets.org/
The eight planets—a tour of the solar system

www.enchantedlearning.com
Enchanted Learning Web site—click on "Astronomy"

stardate.org
Stargazing with the University of Texas McDonald Observatory

pds.jpl.nasa.gov/planets/welcome.htm
Images from NASA's planetary exploration program

Glossary

astronomy the study of stars, planets, and other bodies in space

atmosphere a layer of gas around a large body in space

axis an imaginary line through the middle of an object, from top to bottom

charged carrying electric energy

comet a large ball of rock, ice, gas, and dust which orbits the Sun

core the center, or middle part of a solar system body

craters bowl-shaped hollows in the ground

density a measure of how heavy something is for its size

diameter the distance across

equator an imaginary line around the middle of a globe

gas a substance in which the particles are far apart, not solid or liquid

gravity a force which pulls one body towards another body

hemisphere half of a globe

magnetic field an area where magnetism occurs

mass a measure of how much substance is in something

moons natural bodies which circle around planets or other bodies

orbit *noun* the path a body takes when it moves around another body; *verb* to travel on a path around another body

planet a large, round body which circles the Sun, and does not share its orbit with other bodies (except its moons)

pole the top or bottom of a globe

radiation belts bands in space which contain dangerous rays

radio signals invisible rays

revolve travel around another body

rotates spins

space probe an unmanned spacecraft

star a huge ball of glowing gas in space

telescope an instrument for making faraway objects look bigger and more detailed

trans-Neptunian objects small solar system bodies which orbit the Sun farther out than Neptune, on average

ultraviolet light invisible light

31

Index